Why I Love You Grandmother

The Book I Wrote About Us

The Life Graduate Publishing Group

No part of this book may be scanned, reproduced or distributed in any printed or electronic form without the prior permission of the author or publisher.
Copyright - The Life Graduate Publishing Group 2021 - All Rights Reserved

We love to receive reviews from our customers. If you had the opportunity to provide a review we would greatly appreciate it. Thank you!

Send us an email if you would like to be notified of new books we release via **info@thelifegraduate.com**

Dear Grandmother

Love..........................

THIS BOOK IS WRITTEN FROM MY HEART. I CREATED IT FOR YOU BECAUSE.....

_____

_____

_____

_____

_____

_____

_____

_____

WHEN WE ARE APART GRANDMOTHER, I REALLY MISS...

_____

_____

_____

_____

_____

I LOVE HEARING STORIES ABOUT...

_____
_____
_____
_____

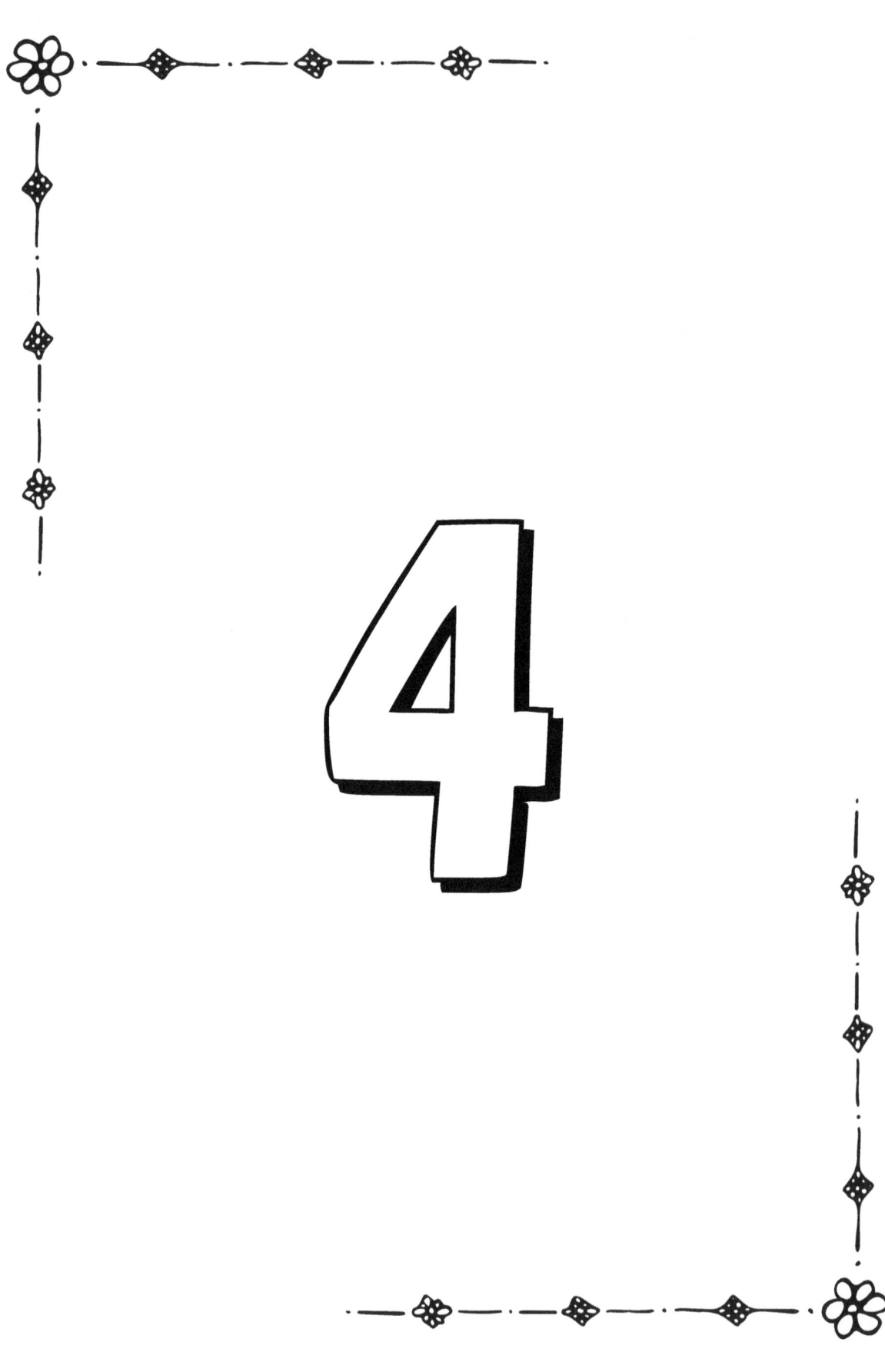

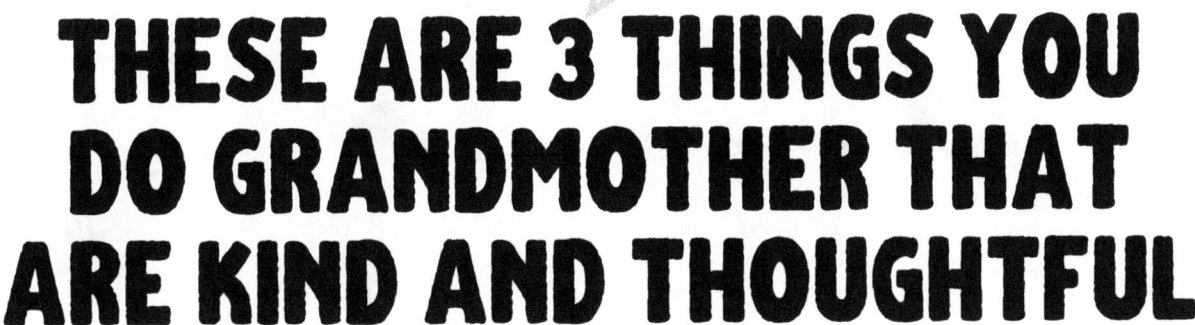

THESE ARE 3 THINGS YOU DO GRANDMOTHER THAT ARE KIND AND THOUGHTFUL

1. _____
   _____

2. _____
   _____

3. _____
   _____

IF I CLOSE MY EYES AND THINK OF SOMETHING SPECIAL WE HAVE DONE TOGETHER, I THINK OF...

_____

_____

_____

_____

I WOULD LOVE TO CREATE A...

FOR YOU

GRANDMOTHER, I WOULD LIKE TO SAY THANK YOU FOR....

_____

_____

_____

_____

I'VE NEVER SAID THIS TO YOU BEFORE, BUT I LOVE IT WHEN YOU...

_____

_____

_____

BECAUSE...

_____

_____

_____

_____

_____

GRANDMOTHER, I REMEMBER THE TIME WE....

YOU MAKE ME LAUGH WHEN....

[ ]

YOU MAKE ME SAD WHEN....

[ ]

YOU MAKE ME SMILE WHEN....

[ ]

IF I COULD TAKE YOU ANYWHERE IN THE WORLD, WE WOULD VISIT..

BOARDING PASS

SEAT: **1A**

DEPARTING LOCATION

ARRIVING LOCATION

WE WOULD VISIT THIS LOCATION BECAUSE

_____

_____

_____

THIS WAS SOMETHING SPECIAL THAT YOU DID FOR ME THAT I WILL NEVER FORGET.....

YOU CAN DO THIS BETTER THAN ANYONE ELSE!

WHEN I HEAR YOUR VOICE, IT MAKES ME FEEL

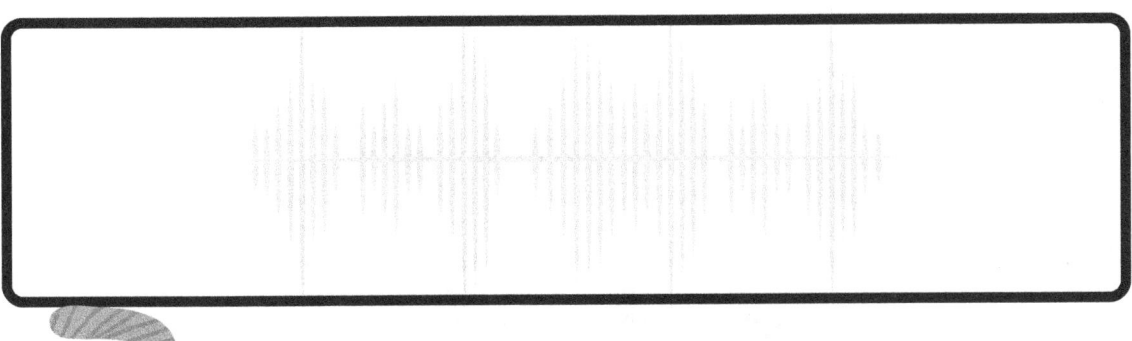

 BECAUSE....

IF I COULD MAKE ONE WISH, I WOULD WISH THAT WE...

GRANDMOTHER, I THINK YOUR SPECIAL 'SUPER-POWER' IS.....

YOU DIDN'T KNOW THIS BUT I...

THESE ARE 3 WORDS THAT BEST DESCRIBE YOU.

1. _____

2. _____

3. _____

GRANDMOTHER, EVERYONE SHOULD BE AS...

_____

AS YOU!

I wrote this book
about us
Grandmother.

Kisses and Hugs

xoxo

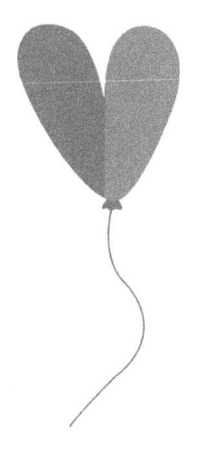
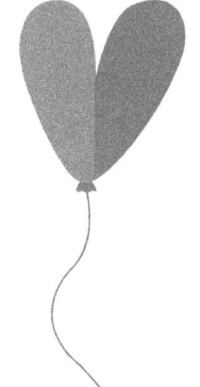

SPECIAL MOMENTS or MEMORIES

Add other special photo's or details here ↙

SPECIAL MOMENTS or MEMORIES

Add other special photo's or details here

 This is a drawing of us

A sample of other books created by
The Life Graduate Publishing Group

www.thelifegraduate.com/bookstore

CPSIA information can be obtained
at www.ICGtesting.com
Printed in the USA
BVHW050831220221
600778BV00010B/1289